Helen Orme is a successful author of fiction and non-fiction, particularly for reluctant and struggling readers. She has written over fifty books for Ransom Publishing.

Helen was a teacher for nearly thirty years. She worked as a Special Educational Needs Co-ordinator in a large comprehensive school, as an advisory teacher for IT and as teacher-in-charge for a pupil referral unit. These experiences have been invaluable in her writing.

The de Ferrers Academy
St Mary's Drive
Burton on Trent
DE13 0LL

StreetWise

The Best Thing Ever
gambling, rebelling against parents

Speed
getting involved in crime

The Newcomer
outsiders, racism, intolerance

I Dare You
taking risks

Fixed It!
cyberbullying

I Can't Help It
smoking

Best Mates
coping with peer pressure

Everyone Does It
cheating

Just Try It!
drugs

Don't Believe Her
sex

Just One More
alcohol

Taking Responsibility
conflicting priorities: home and school

Everyone Does It

Helen Orme

Ransom

Street**Wise**

Everyone Does It
by Helen Orme

Published by Ransom Publishing Ltd.
Radley House, 8 St. Cross Road, Winchester, Hampshire SO23 9HX, UK
www.ransom.co.uk

ISBN   978 184167 349 3
First published in 2014

Copyright © 2014 Ransom Publishing Ltd.
Text copyright © 2014 Helen Orme
Cover photograph copyright © addimage. Image page 6 copyright © larslentz.

A CIP catalogue record of this book is available from the British Library.

All rights reserved. No part of this publication may be reproduced, stored in a retrieval system, or transmitted, in any form or by any means, electronic, mechanical, photocopying, recording or otherwise, without the prior permission of the publishers.

The right of Helen Orme to be identified as the author of this Work has been asserted by her in accordance with sections 77 and 78 of the Copyright, Design and Patents Act 1988.

CONTENTS

1	Found Out	7
2	The Letter	11
3	A Bad Feeling	16
4	Fatal Error	21
5	Everyone Does It	24

Questions on the Story	27
Discussion Points	30
Activities	33

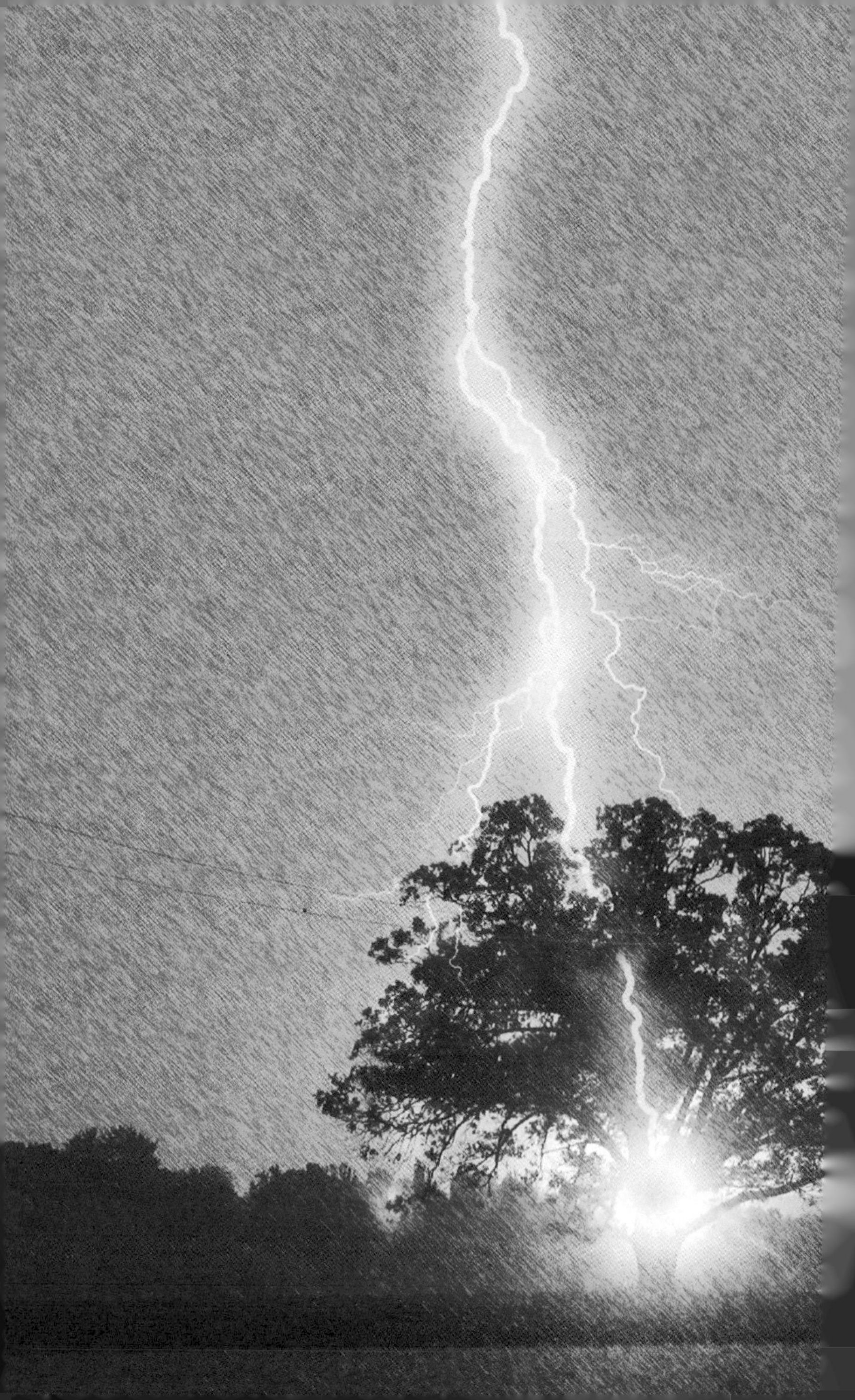

ONE

Found Out

'Ben, I really thought you had more sense.'

Mrs Tapping was Ben's History teacher.

She had asked Ben to stay behind after

class. Ben's History coursework folder was open on the desk.

'What do you mean?'

'Ben, I think you know exactly what I mean. This essay on World War Two. These are not your own words, are they?'

'Well … '

'Ben, I'm going to stop you there, before you start lying to me. This phrase here. I put it into Google and found where you got it from. In fact, I found the whole paragraph you used.

'Ben, you must remember what I said to the class when you started putting your coursework together. It must be your own words.

'You can use the Internet for research, but you mustn't cut and paste someone else's text.

'I'm sorry Ben, but this is cheating, and

it's a serious matter.

'I'm sorry to tell you that you have failed the course. I will be writing to your parents to explain why.'

TWO

The Letter

Two days later.

Ben wasn't looking forward to going home.

He knew that Mrs Tapping's letter would have arrived.

He knew he should have owned up to his parents before they got the letter, but he just couldn't do it.

Life was difficult at home just then.

His mum had just lost her job and money was tight. This had led to rows.

*****

It was really bad.

Simon, Ben's younger brother, was sent

upstairs to play on his computer.

Then the lecture began.

'Ben, how could you? You must have known it was cheating!'

'Everyone does it.'

'Ben, that's just not true. How could you be so stupid? You must have known you would be found out!'

And on and on.

Ben tried to explain why he had done it

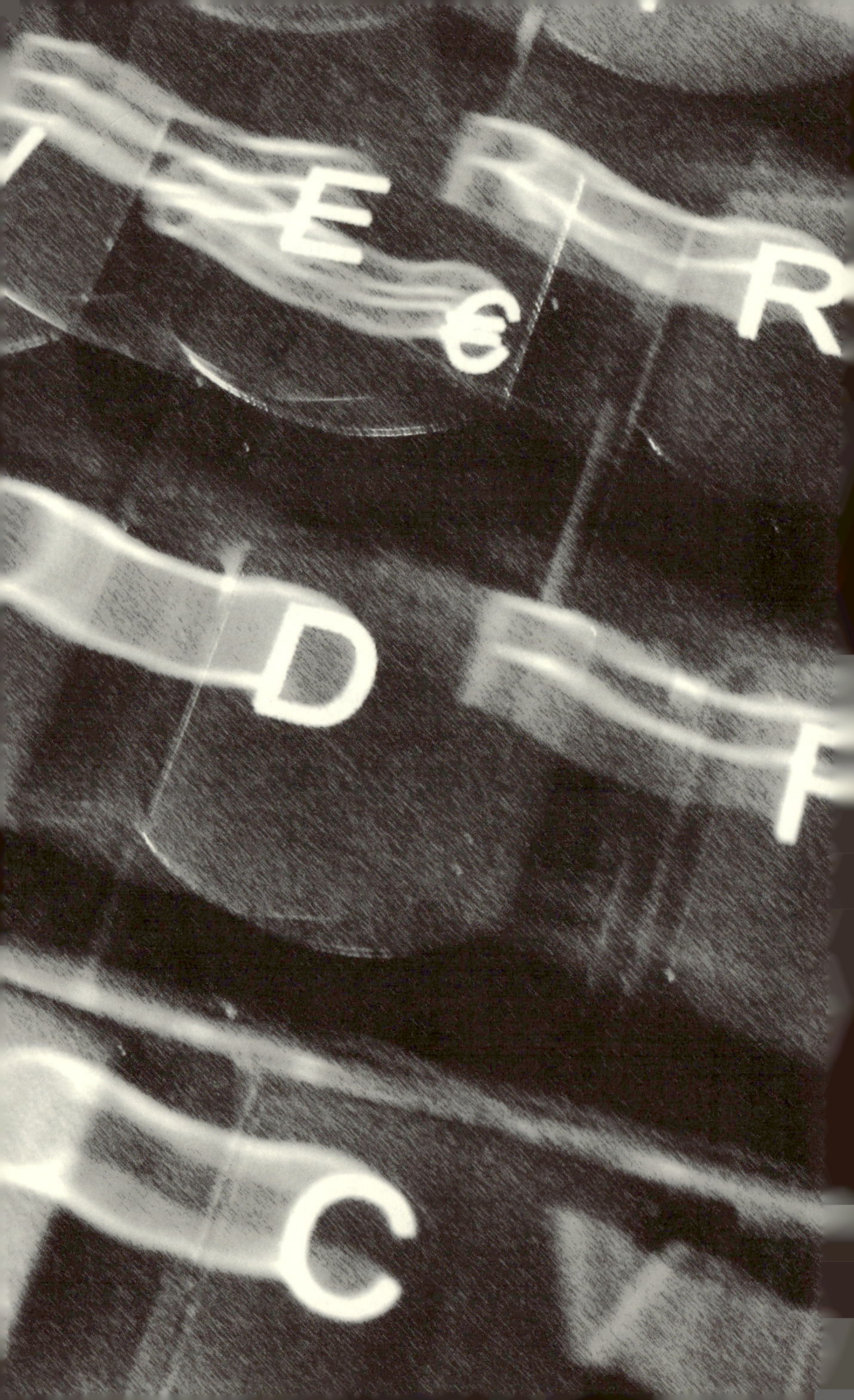
E
€
R
D
F
C

– so much work to get done, so little time.

But they wouldn't listen.

Perhaps it was just as well.

They might have asked, 'And how much time do you spend on the computer playing games or chatting to friends?'

And that was a question he really didn't want to answer.

THREE

A Bad Feeling

Ben had promised faithfully that he had only cut and pasted stuff for his History coursework.

Not for his other subjects.

He had a bad feeling though that some

of his Geography coursework might be a bit dodgy as well.

Luckily, he had another week before it had to be handed in.

He kept his work on a flash drive. This meant he could work on it at school and at home.

School was closed on Friday, so he had the whole day at home to sort it.

*****

Mum was working on her laptop downstairs.

She was looking for jobs and applying for them online.

Ben switched on his machine and started work.

... He was sure he had written that bit ... Hmm, maybe not ...

... He had no idea what that word meant! ...

Employ

*****

After a while, he saved his work back to the flash drive.

Better check Facebook. Mustn't spend too long on it, though …

FOUR

Fatal Error

Half an hour later, and Ben was still on Facebook.

There was a new game there that one of his mates had sent him a message about. He knew it was stupid, but it was really addictive, and he'd already got a brilliant score.

Anyway, he was entitled to some down time, wasn't he?

He looked at the clock. Was that really the time? He logged out and tried to open his work file. A message came up on the screen.

FATAL SYSTEM ERROR.

The screen went blue.

Ben turned the machine off, then on again, but it wouldn't power up.

FIVE

Everyone Does It

Downstairs, Mum had finished working on her computer. She was putting her coat on ready to go out.

'Mum, my laptop's died! I've really got to get this work done! Can I use yours?'

Mum sighed. She hated other people using her laptop.

'OK Ben, but no playing games. Promise? I've got to go out for a bit. I haven't shut it down yet.'

Mum went out and Ben plugged in his flash drive. Straight away the screen lit up. Mum hadn't closed the program she was using.

Ben glanced at it. It was an application

for a job in an office. Mum had been working on her C.V.

He'd better check that she had saved the file. Idly, he read it. Then he wished he hadn't.

Some of the things his mum had said were true, but he knew his Mum hadn't done all the things she said she had. She had made it up. She was lying to get the job.

But then, everyone does it, don't they?

Questions on the Story

- Why did Ben fail the course?

- Why did Ben's mum not tell the truth in her C.V.?

◆ Why didn't Ben have enough time to do the work properly?

Discussion Points

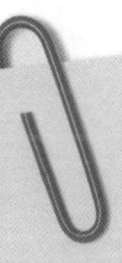

- Ben cut and pasted his coursework from the Internet. Why isn't this a good idea?

(Coursework is part of an exam.)

Wise

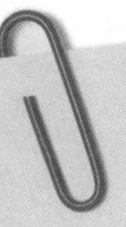

- How should you use the Internet to help with your work? What problems might there be?

- *Does* everyone do it?

Activities

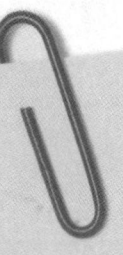

- Imagine that Ben and his mum have another row, and Ben accuses her of cheating.

   Write their conversation. This could be in direct speech or a play script.

- Write a list of rules for using the Internet for coursework.

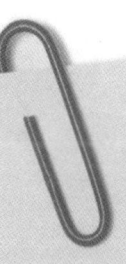

- Are computer games good, or just a waste of time? Use this plan for a piece of writing:

Arguments for computer games.

Arguments against computer games.

- Give your own opinion on computer games and explain why.